transcribed **horns**

NOTE-FOR-NOTE TRANSCRIPTIONS · FROM THE ORIGINAL RECORDINGS

POP/ROCK
HORN SECTION

ISBN 978-1-4234-4678-1

HAL•LEONARD®
CORPORATION
7777 W. BLUEMOUND RD. P.O. BOX 13819 MILWAUKEE, WI 53213

For all works contained herein:
Unauthorized copying, arranging, adapting, recording or public performance is an infringement of copyright.
Infringers are liable under the law.

Visit Hal Leonard Online at
www.halleonard.com

BRIGHT SIDE OF THE ROAD

Words and Music by
VAN MORRISON

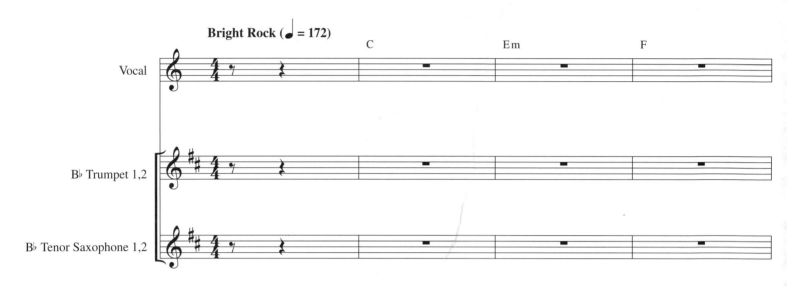

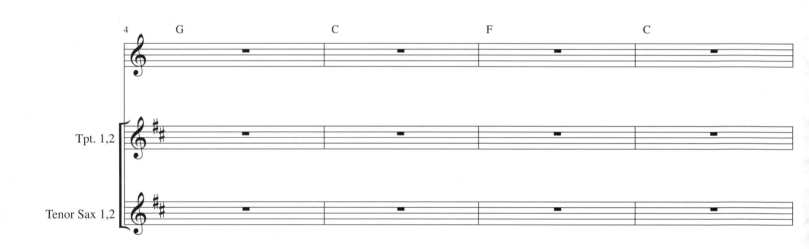

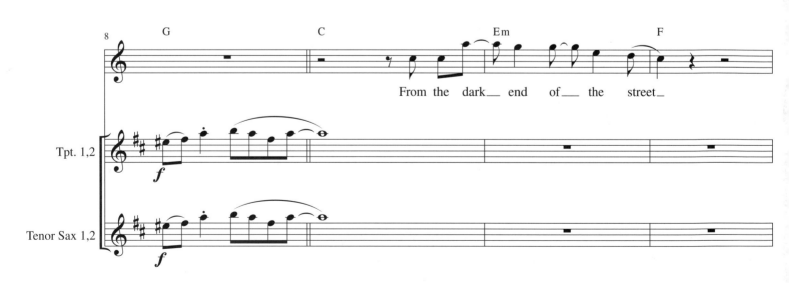

From the dark__ end of__ the street__

Copyright © 1979 ESSENTIAL MUSIC
All Rights in the U.S. and Canada Controlled and Administered by UNIVERSAL - SONGS OF POLYGRAM INTERNATIONAL, INC.
All Rights Reserved   Used by Permission

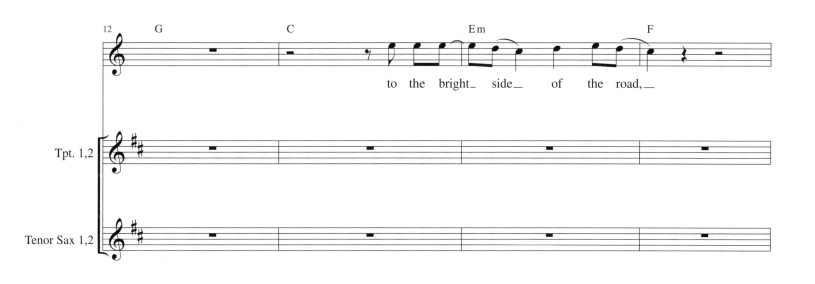

to the bright side of the road,

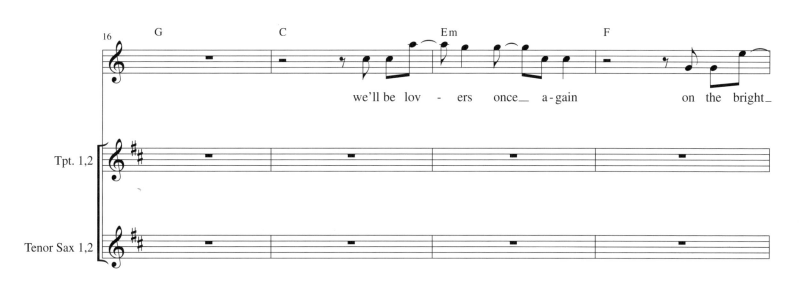

we'll be lov - ers once a - gain on the bright

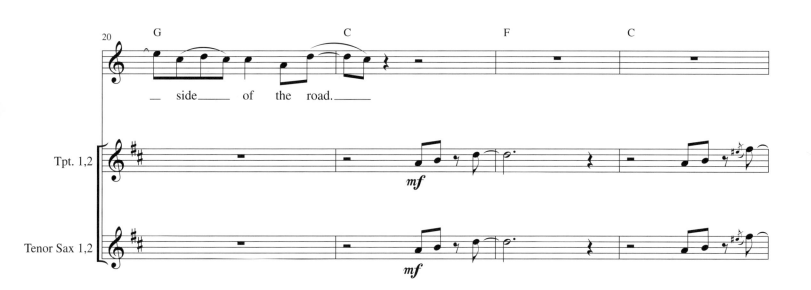

side of the road.

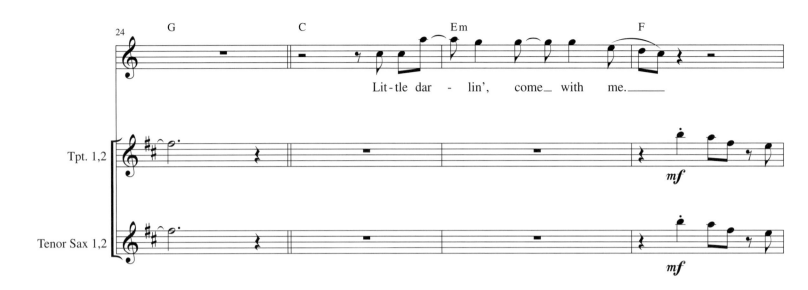

Lit-tle dar - lin', come_ with me._

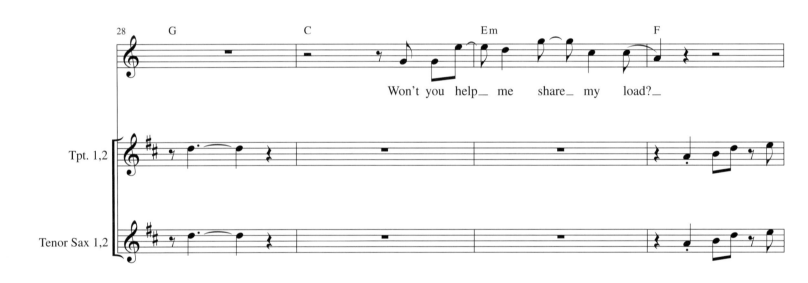

Won't you help_ me share_ my load?_

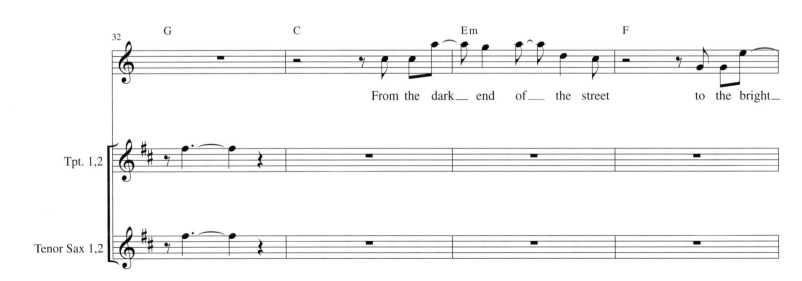

From the dark_ end of_ the street to the bright_

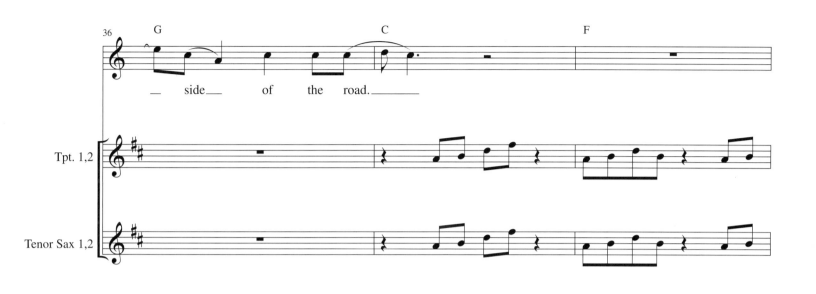

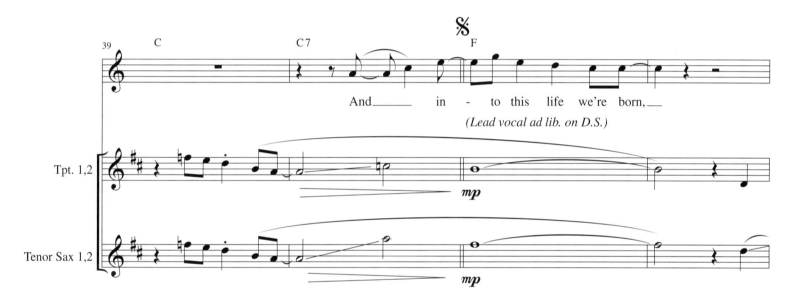

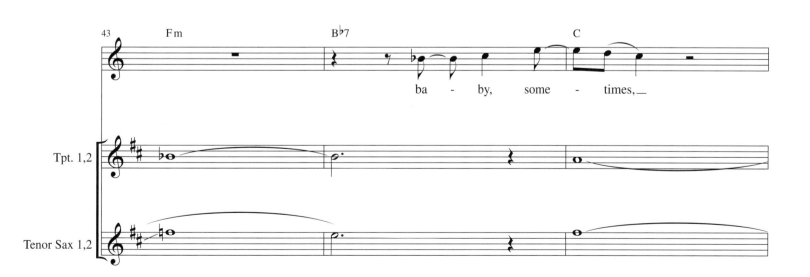

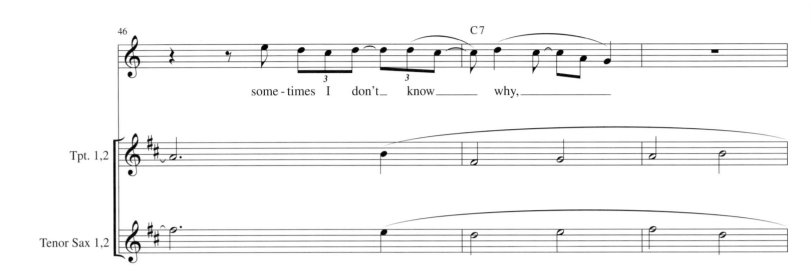

some - times I don't_ know_____ why,_____

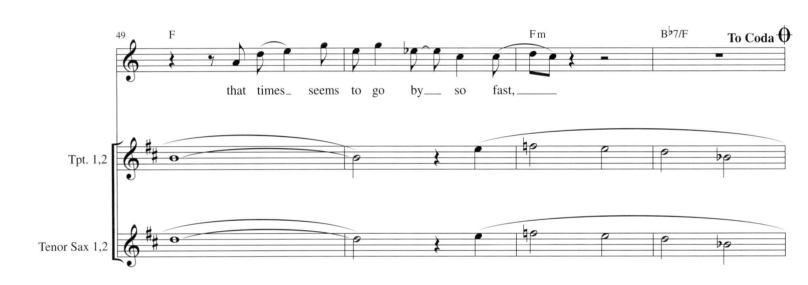

that times_ seems to go by___ so fast,_____

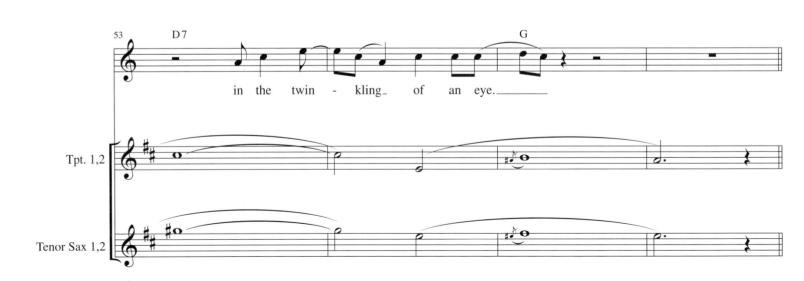

in the twin - kling_ of an eye._____

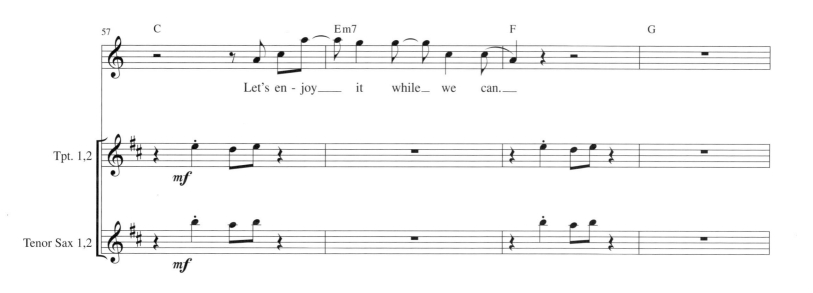

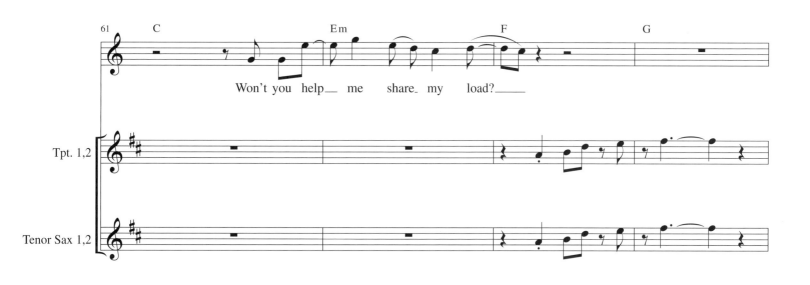

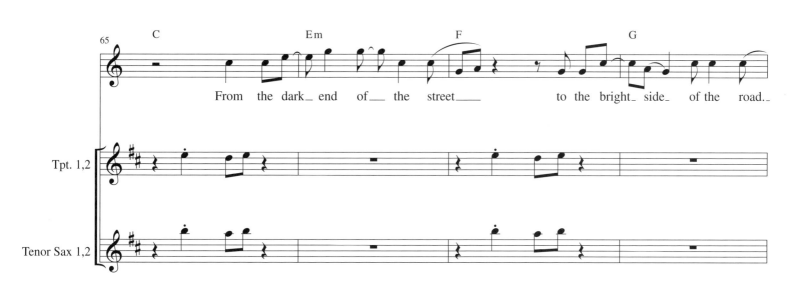

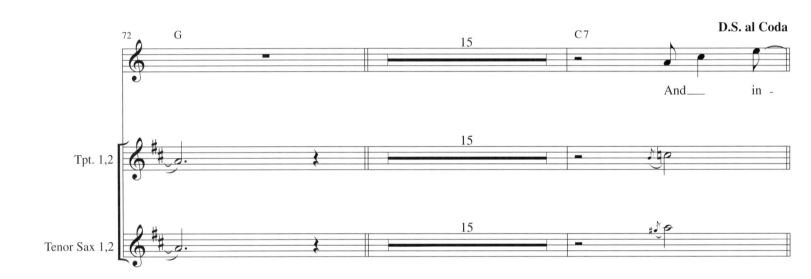

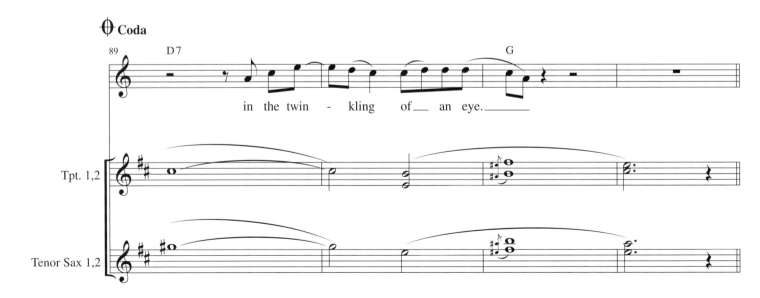

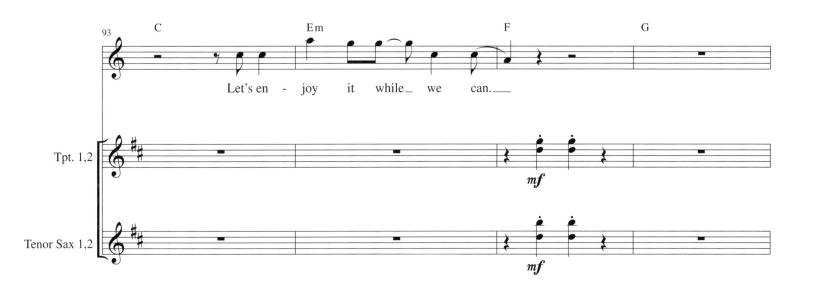

Let's en - joy it while__ we can.__

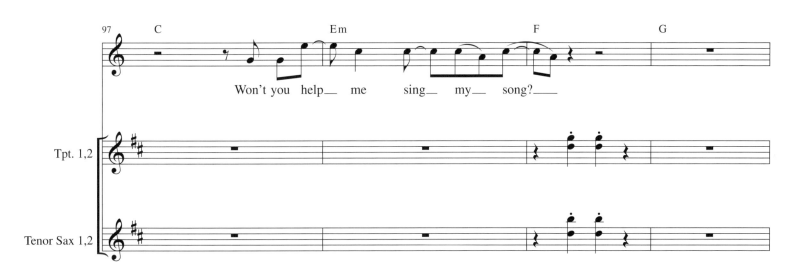

Won't you help__ me sing__ my__ song?__

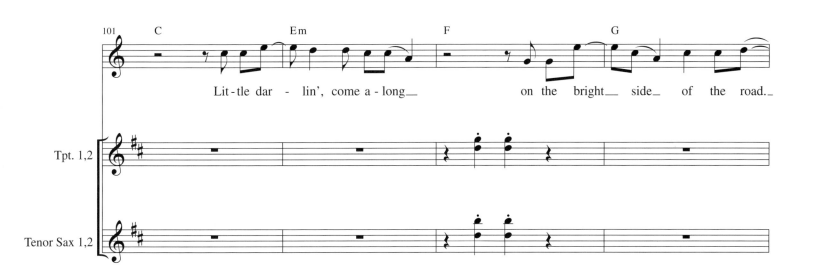

Lit - tle dar - lin', come a - long__ on the bright__ side__ of the road.__

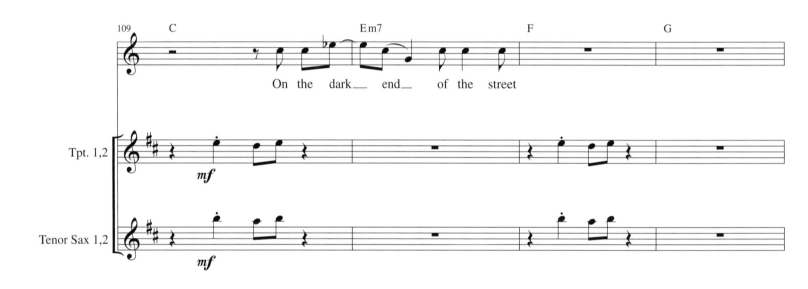

On the dark___ end___ of the street

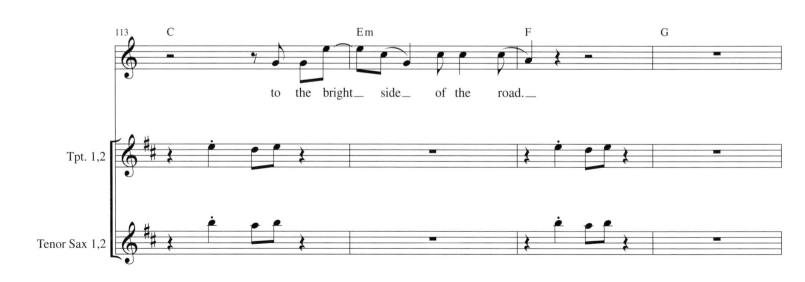

to the bright___ side___ of the road.___

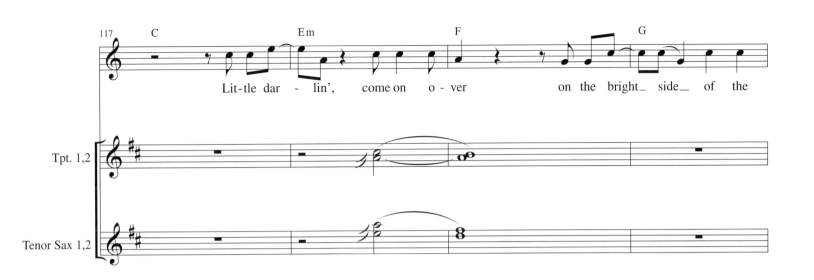

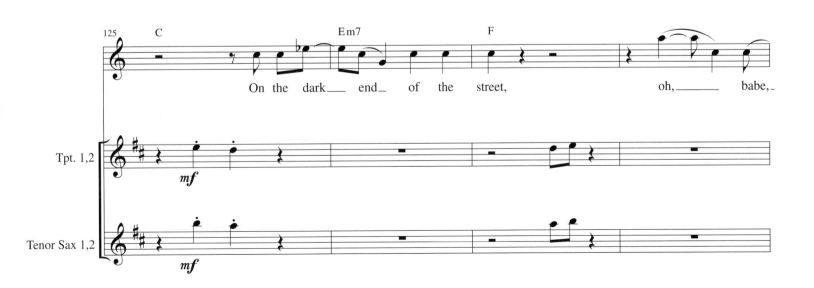

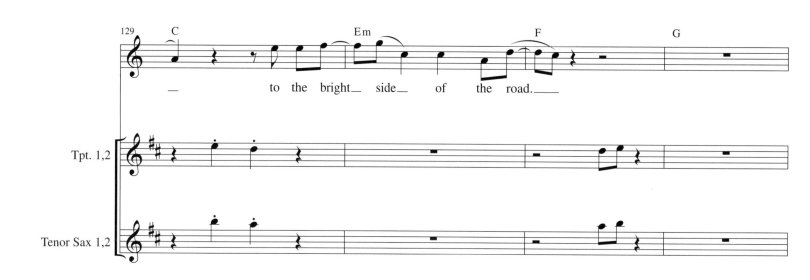

to the bright side of the road.

We'll be lov - ers once a - gain, on the bright side of the road.

Well, we'll be,

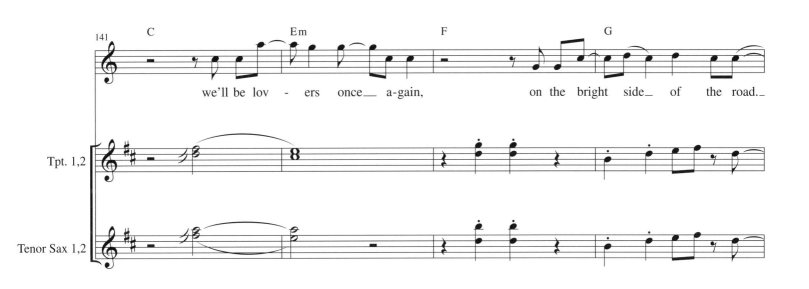

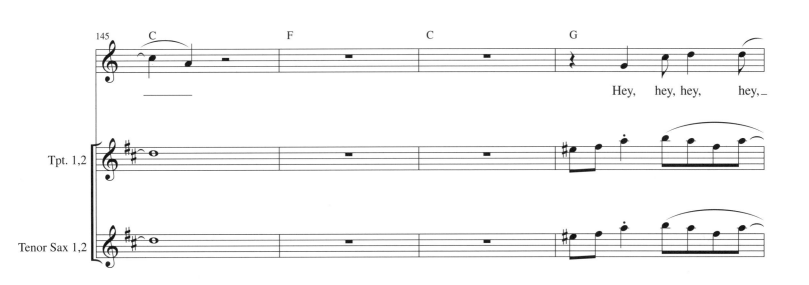

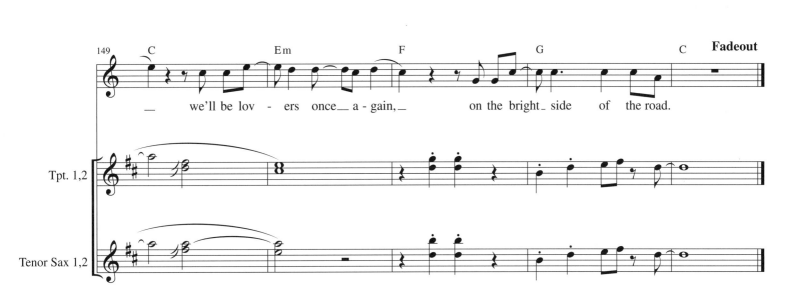

HIGHER LOVE

Words and Music by WILL JENNINGS
and STEVE WINWOOD

Copyright © 1986 BLUE SKY RIDER SONGS and F.S. MUSIC LTD.
All Rights for BLUE SKY RIDER SONGS Administered by IRVING MUSIC, INC.
All Rights for F.S. MUSIC LTD. Administered by WARNER-TAMERLANE PUBLISHING CORP.
All Rights Reserved Used by Permission

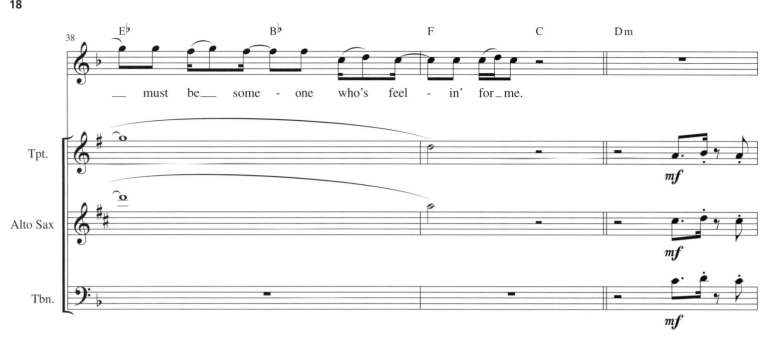

must be___ some - one who's feel - in' for___ me.

D.S. al Coda

Coda

Bring me a high - er___ love.   Bring me a high - er___ love,

Repeat 3 times and Fade

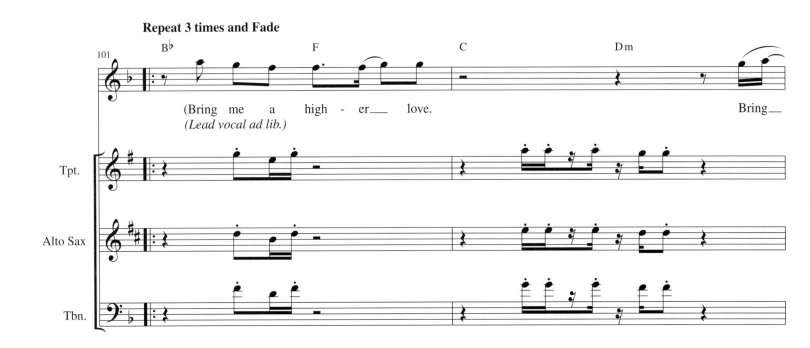

Fadeout (3rd time)

HOT HOT HOT

Words and Music by
ALPHONSUS CASSELL

Copyright © 1983, 1987 Chrysalis Music Ltd.
All Rights in the U.S. and Canada Administered by Chrysalis Music
All Rights Reserved   Used by Permission

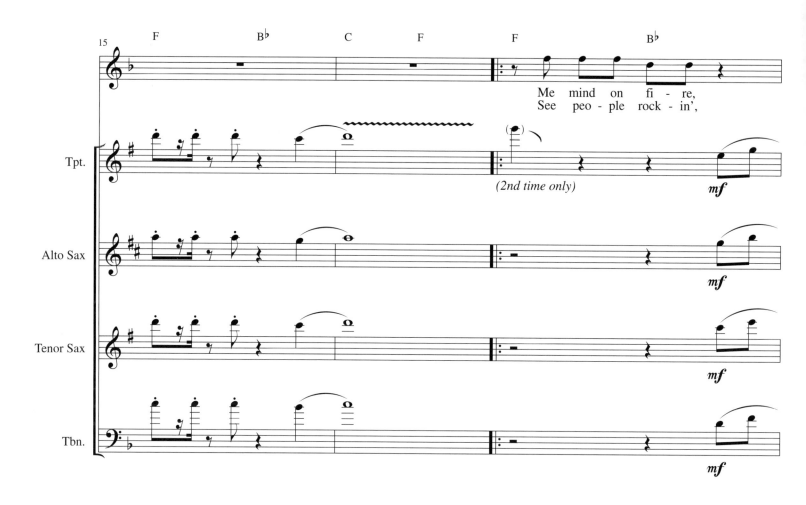

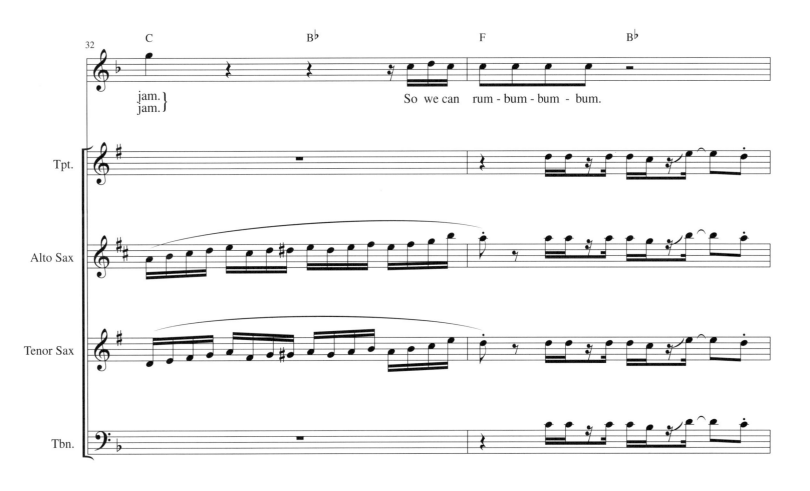

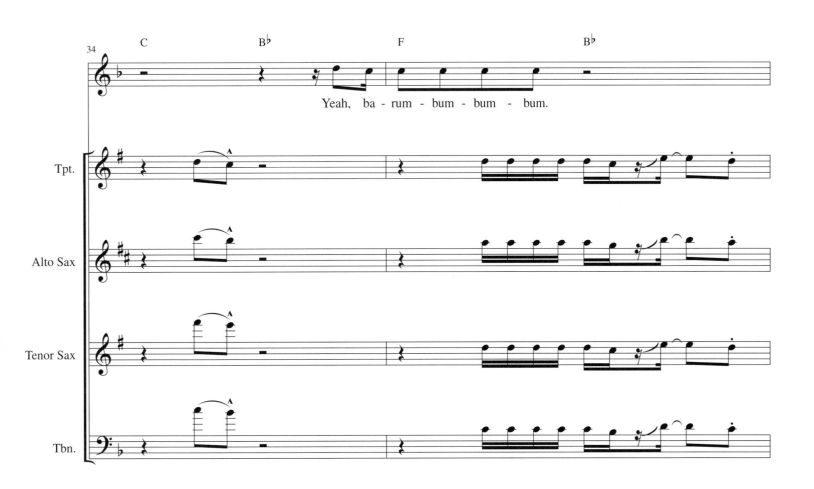

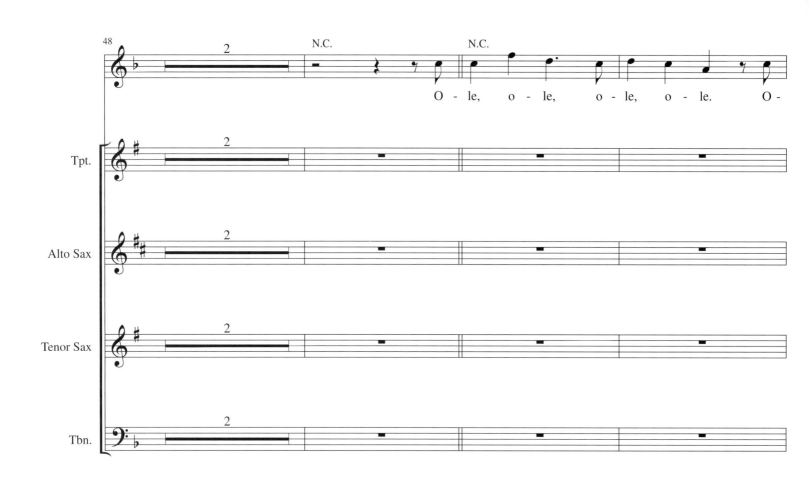

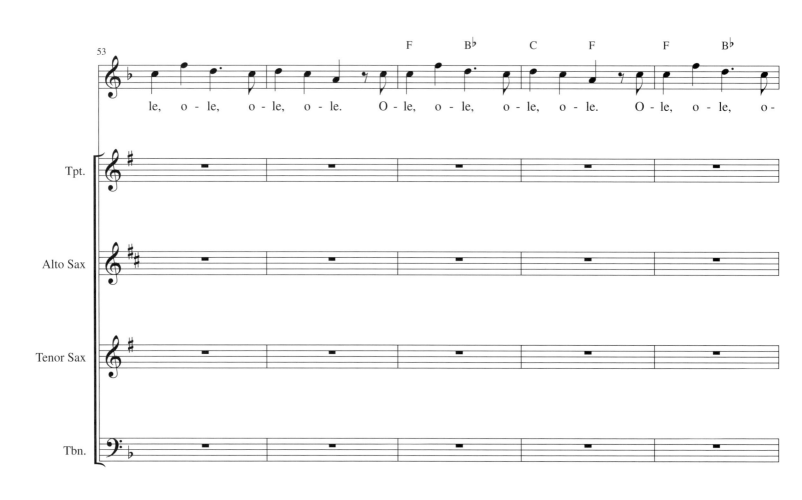

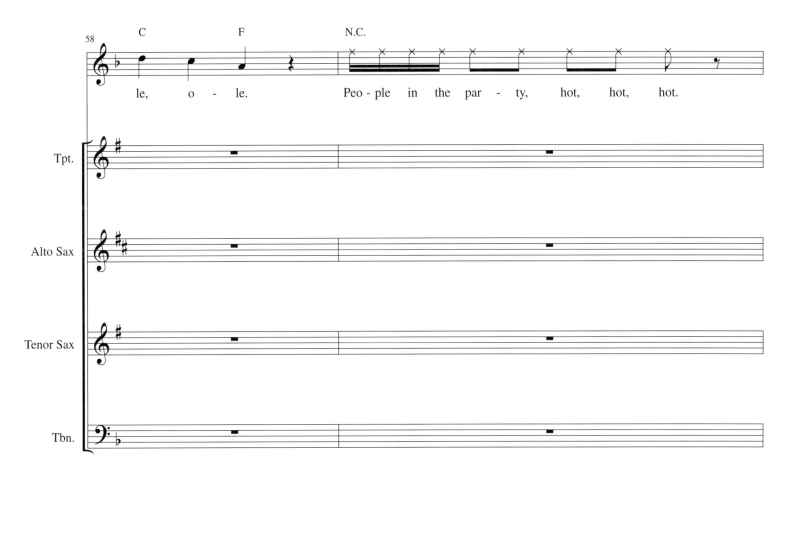

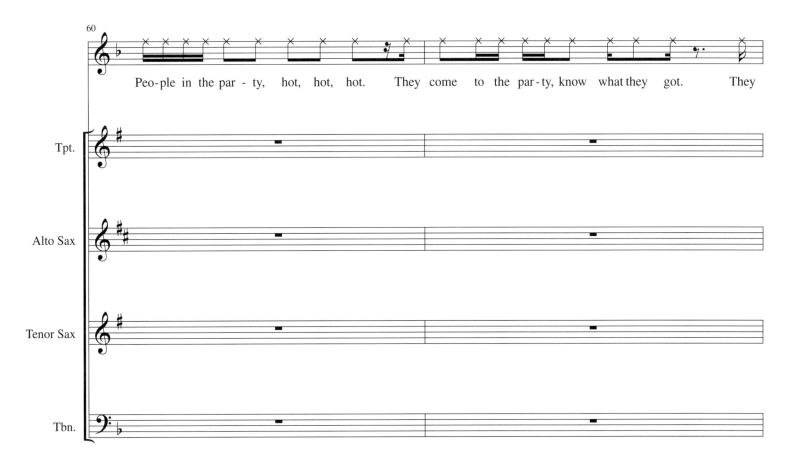

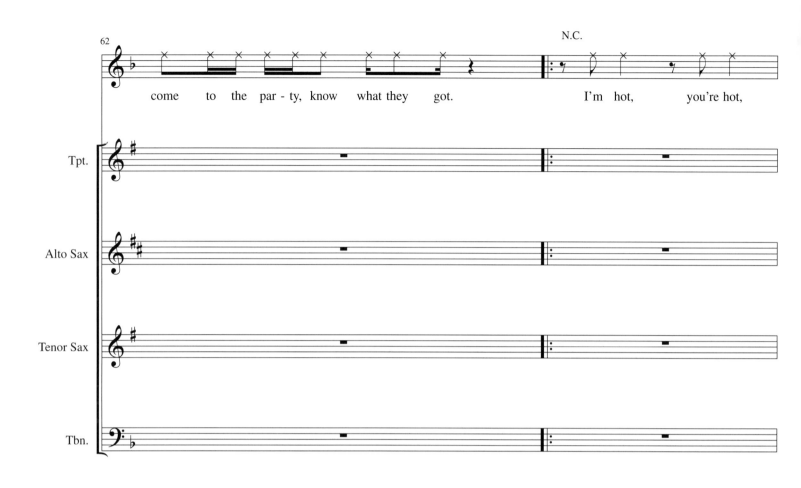

come to the par-ty, know what they got. I'm hot, you're hot,

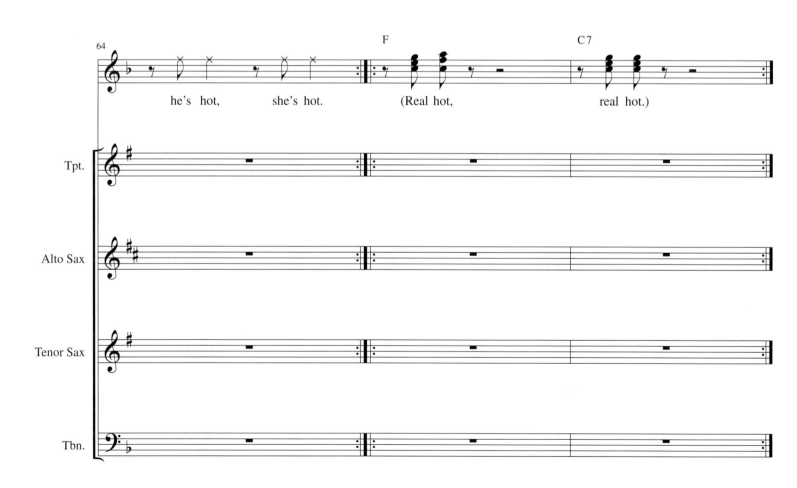

he's hot, she's hot. (Real hot, real hot.)

38

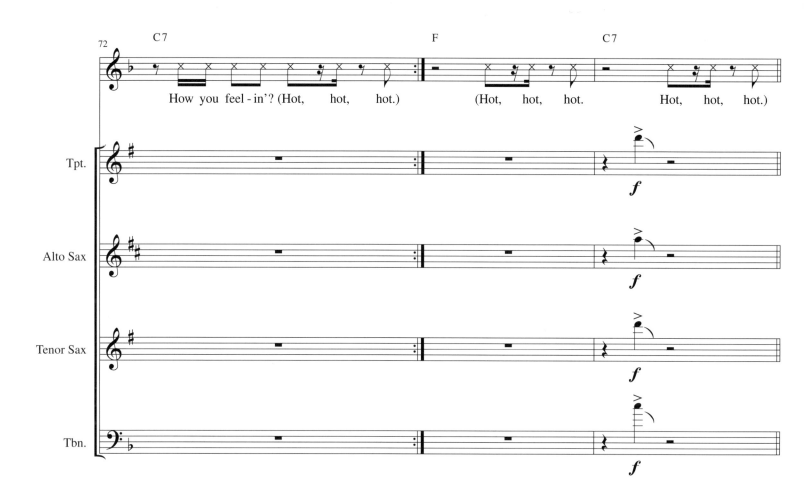

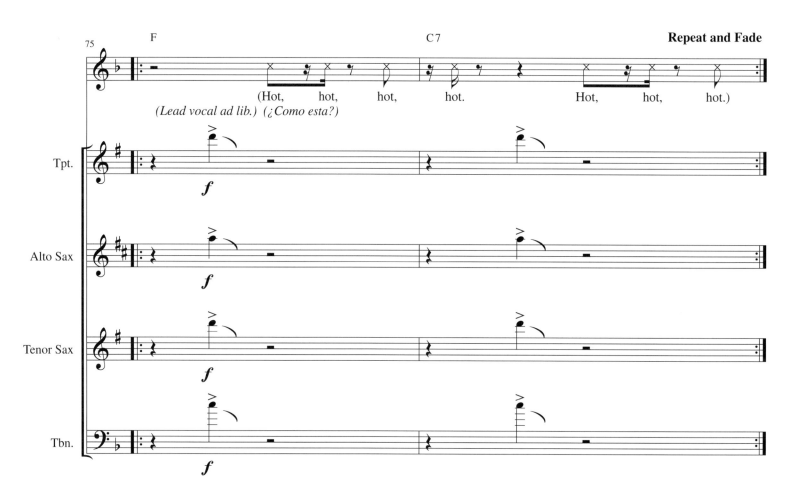

THE IMPRESSION THAT I GET

Words and Music by DICKY BARRETT
and JOE GITTLEMAN

© 1997 EMI APRIL MUSIC INC. and BOSSTONES MUSIC
All Rights Controlled and Administered by EMI APRIL MUSIC INC.
All Rights Reserved   International Copyright Secured   Used by Permission

JUMP, JIVE AN' WAIL

Words and Music by
LOUIS PRIMA

© 1956 (Renewed 1984) LGL MUSIC INC.
All Rights Controlled and Administered by EMI APRIL MUSIC INC.
All Rights Reserved   International Copyright Secured   Used by Permission

knows how to jive__ and wail.__

Jack and Jill__ went up__ the hill to__ get a pail.__

LIVIN' LA VIDA LOCA

Words and Music by ROBI ROSA
and DESMOND CHILD

Copyright © 1999 UNIVERSAL - POLYGRAM INTERNATIONAL PUBLISHING, INC., DESMOPHOBIA and A PHANTOM VOX PUBLISHING
All Rights for DESMOPHOBIA Controlled and Administered by UNIVERSAL - POLYGRAM INTERNATIONAL PUBLISHING, INC.
All Rights for A PHANTOM VOX PUBLISHING Controlled and Administered by WARNER-TAMERLANE PUBLISHING CORP.
All Rights Reserved   Used by Permission

liv - in' la vi - da___ lo - ca.

MAGICAL MYSTERY TOUR

Words and Music by JOHN LENNON
and PAUL McCARTNEY

(Spoken:) Roll up, roll up for the Magical Mystery Tour. Step right this way.

Roll up,_____ roll up for the mys-

Copyright © 1967 Sony/ATV Music Publishing LLC
Copyright Renewed
All Rights Administered by Sony/ATV Music Publishing LLC, 8 Music Square West, Nashville, TN 37203
International Copyright Secured   All Rights Reserved

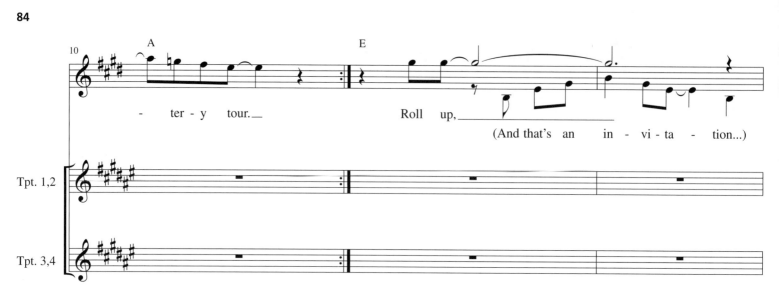

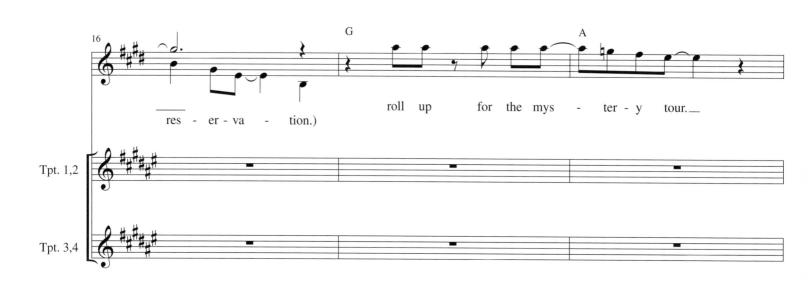

PEG

Words and Music by WALTER BECKER
and DONALD FAGEN

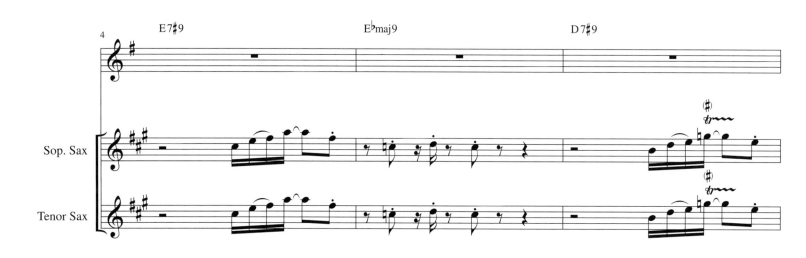

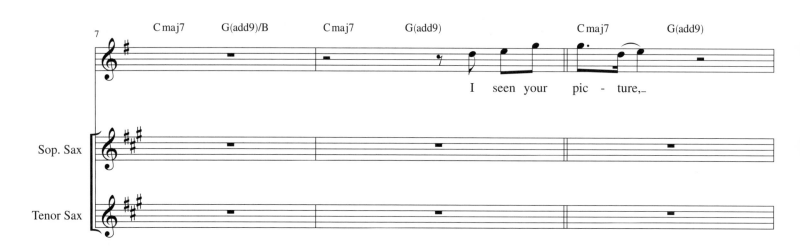

I seen your pic - ture,_

Copyright © 1977 UNIVERSAL MUSIC CORP.
Copyright Renewed
All Rights Reserved   Used by Permission

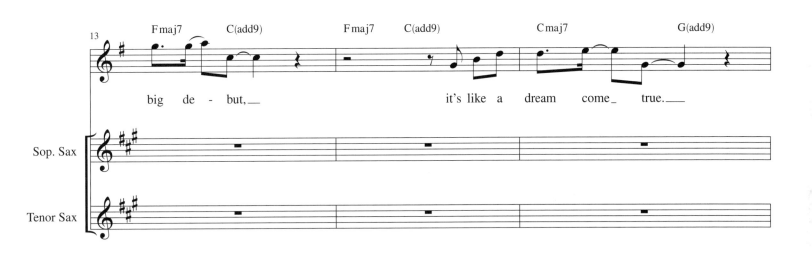

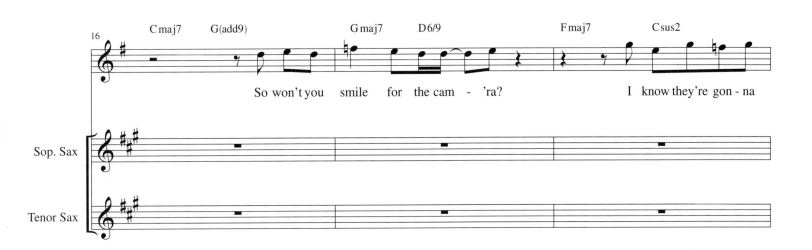

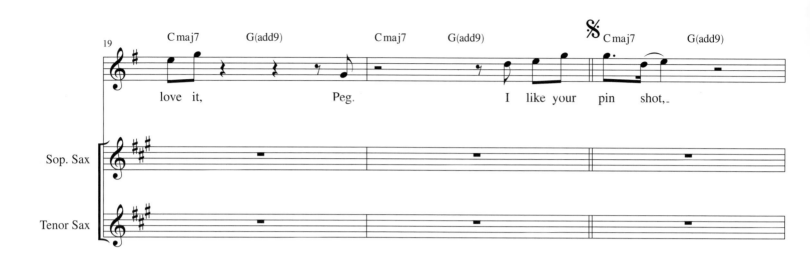

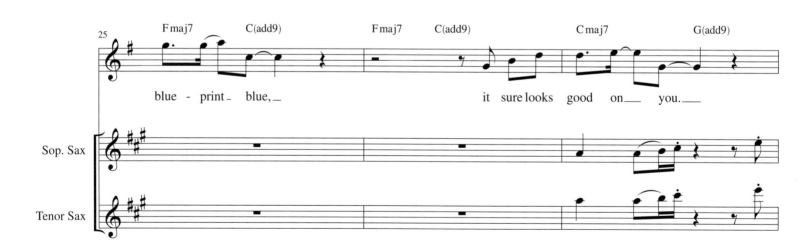

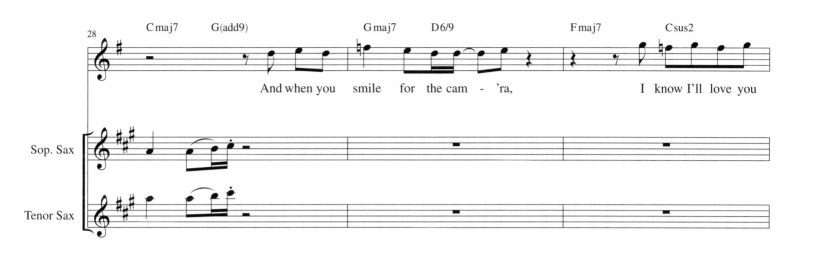

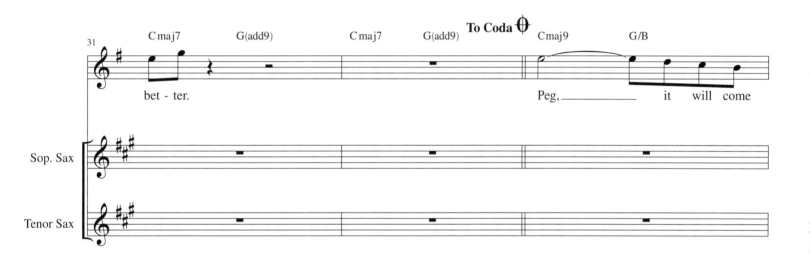

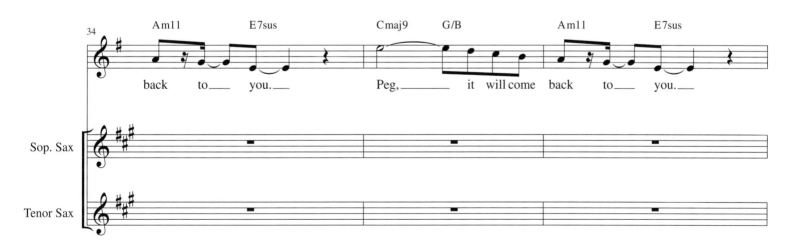

Then the shut-ter falls, you see it all in 3 - D.

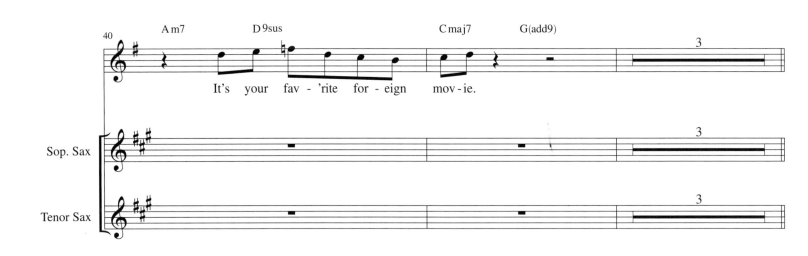

It's your fav - 'rite for - eign mov - ie.

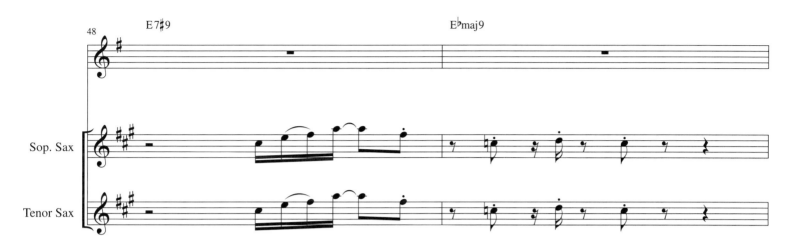

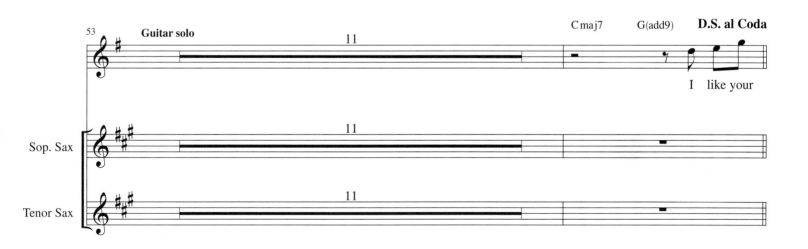

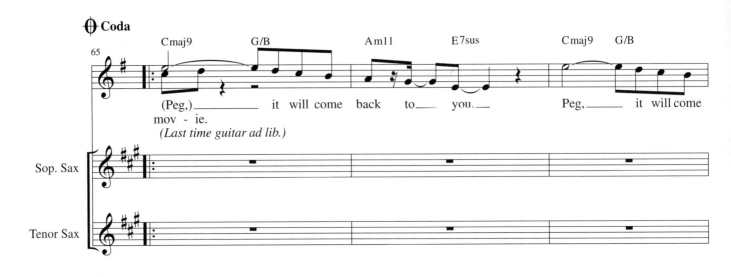

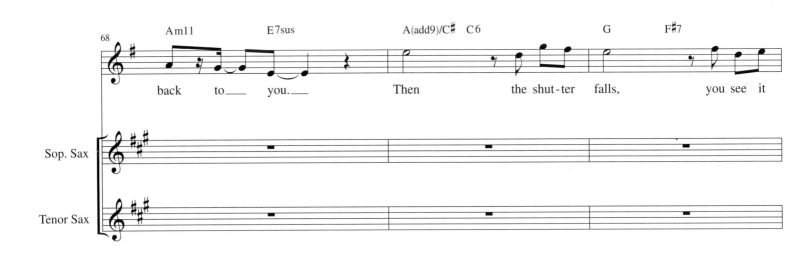

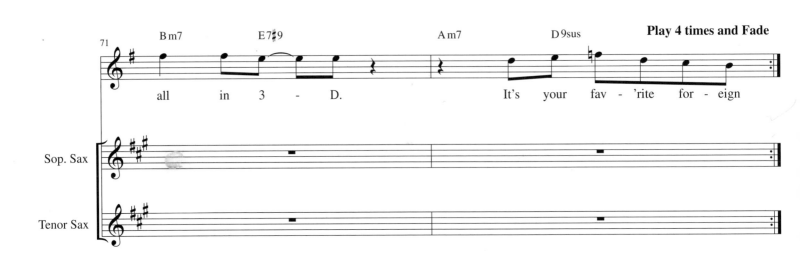

SMOOTH

Words by ROB THOMAS
Music by ROB THOMAS and ITAAL SHUR

© 1999 EMI BLACKWOOD MUSIC INC., BIDNIS, INC. and ITAAL SHUR MUSIC
All Rights for BIDNIS, INC. Controlled and Administered by EMI BLACKWOOD MUSIC INC.
All Rights Reserved   International Copyright Secured   Used by Permission

SPINNING WHEEL

Words and Music by
DAVID CLAYTON THOMAS

© 1968 (Renewed 1996) EMI BLACKWOOD MUSIC INC. and BAY MUSIC LTD.
All Rights Controlled and Administered by EMI BLACKWOOD MUSIC INC.
All Rights Reserved   International Copyright Secured   Used by Permission

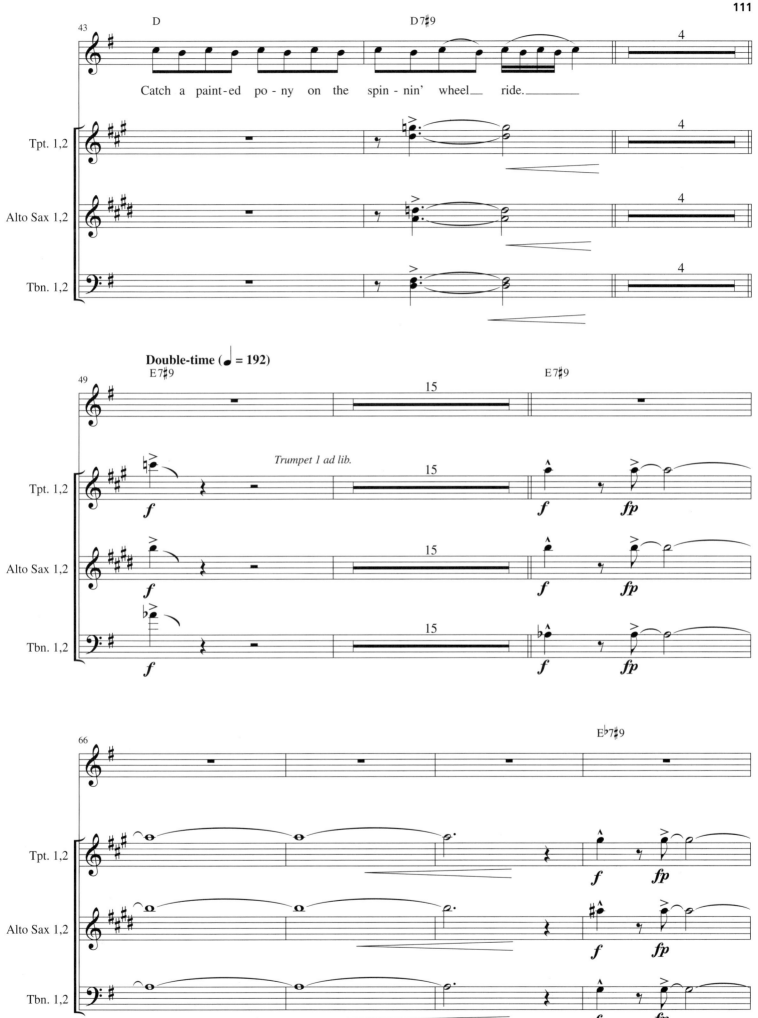

Catch a paint-ed po - ny on the spin - nin' wheel___ ride.___

(Lead vocal tacet on repeat)

SUSSUDIO

Words and Music by
PHIL COLLINS

© 1984 PHILIP COLLINS LTD. and HIT & RUN MUSIC (PUBLISHING) LTD.
All Rights Controlled and Administered by EMI APRIL MUSIC INC.
All Rights Reserved   International Copyright Secured   Used by Permission

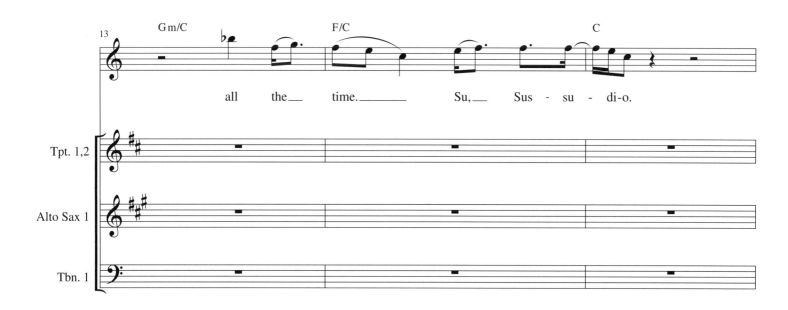

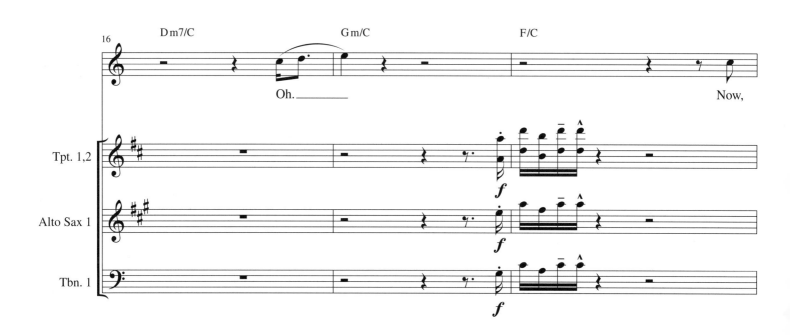

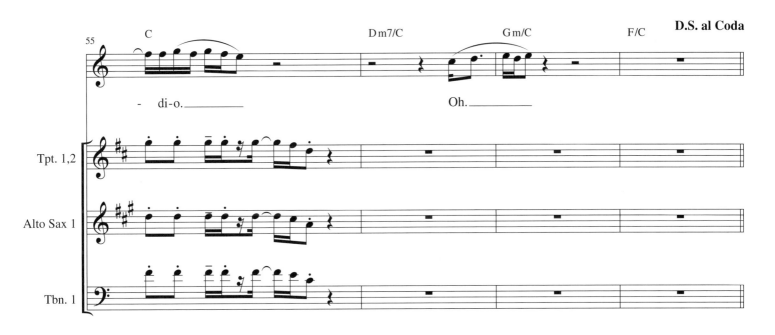

Ah,   she's all I   need,__   all   my life.

94
2.
C
Dm7/C
B♭/C
F/C
N.C.
- di-o. Su - di-o, Su, Sus - su - di-o.
Tpt. 1,2
Alto Sax 1
Tbn. 1
Alternate horns (overdubbed)
Tpt. 3,4
Alto Sax 2
Tbn. 2
Alternate horns 2 (overdubbed)
Tpt. 5,6
Alto Sax 3
Tbn. 3

128

Just say the

25 OR 6 TO 4

Words and Music by
ROBERT LAMM

Copyright © 1970 Lamminations Music and Aurelius Music
Copyright Renewed
All Rights Reserved

VEHICLE

Words and Music by
JAMES M. PETERIK

Copyright © 1969 by BALD MEDUSA MUSIC
Copyright Renewed
International Copyright Secured   All Rights Reserved

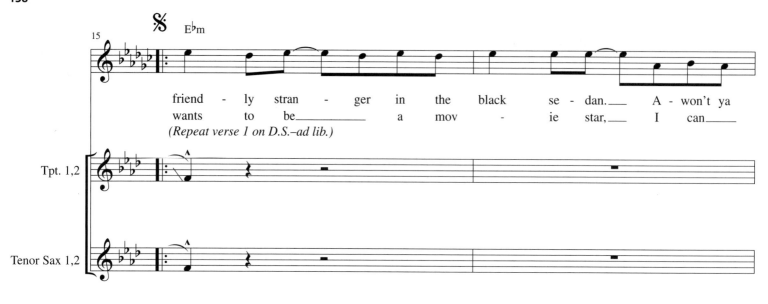

friend - ly stran - ger in the black se - dan.___ A - won't ya
wants to be___ a mov - ie star,___ I can___

(Repeat verse 1 on D.S.–ad lib.)

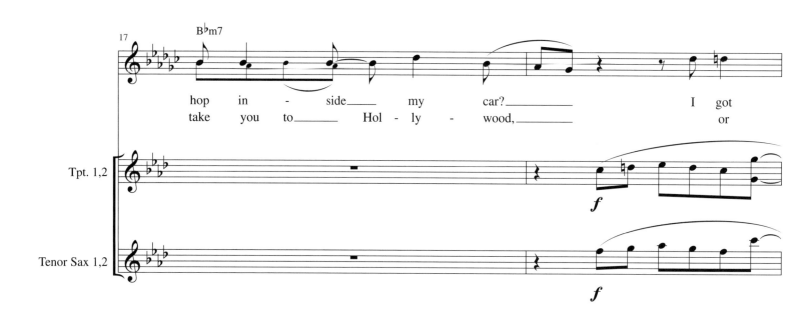

hop in - side___ my car?___ I got
take you to___ Hol - ly - wood,___ or

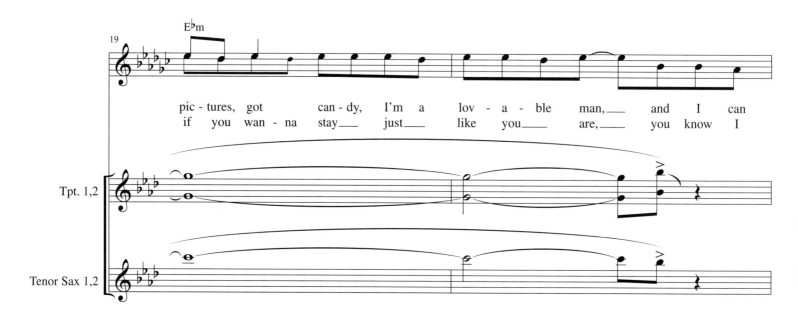

pic - tures, got can - dy, I'm a lov - a - ble man,___ and I can
if you wan - na stay___ just___ like you___ are,___ you know I

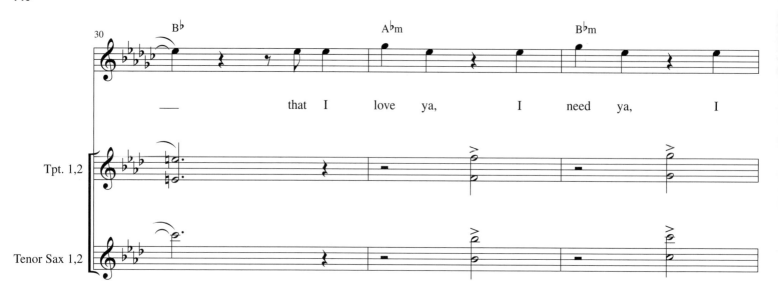

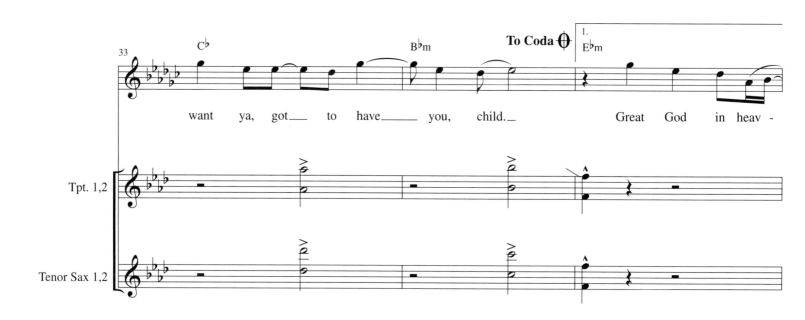

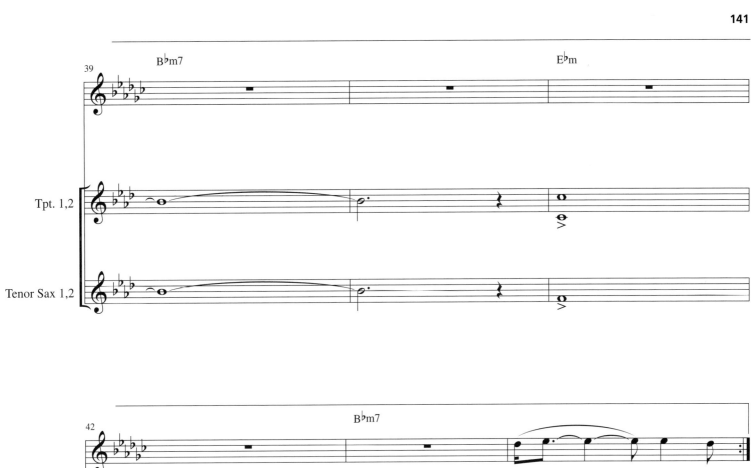

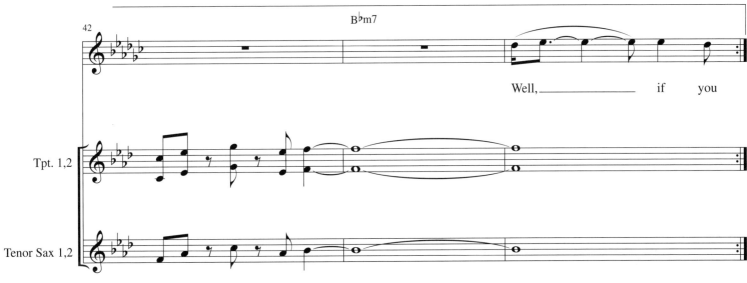

Well,_____ if you

Great God in heav - en, you know__ I love_____

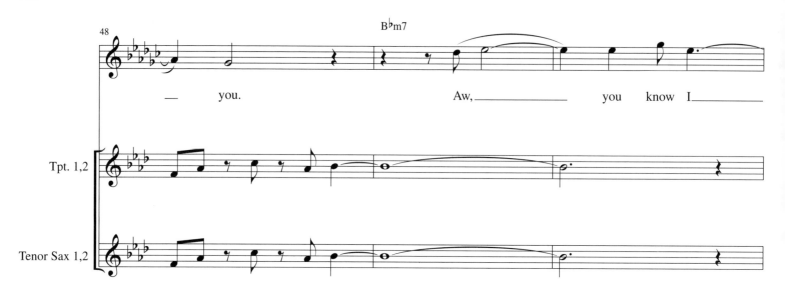

you. Aw,_____ you know I_____

— do._____

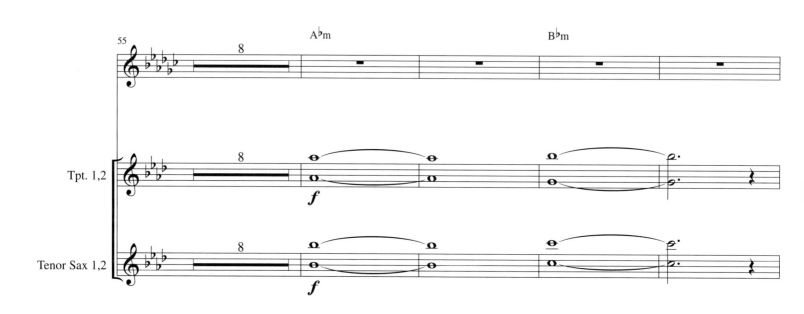

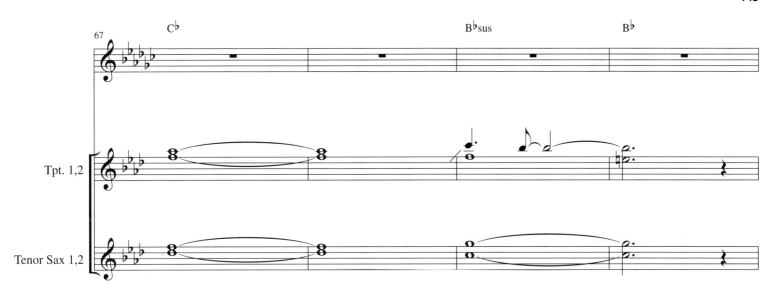

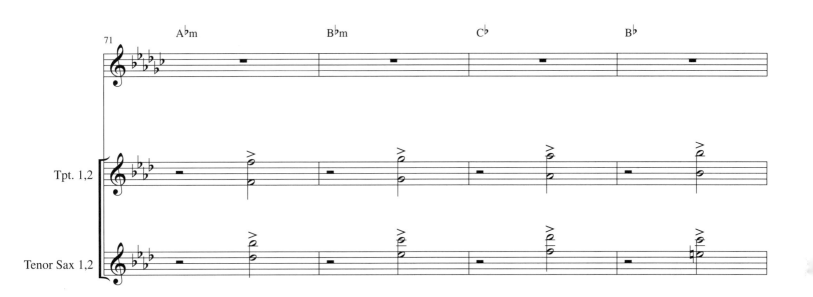

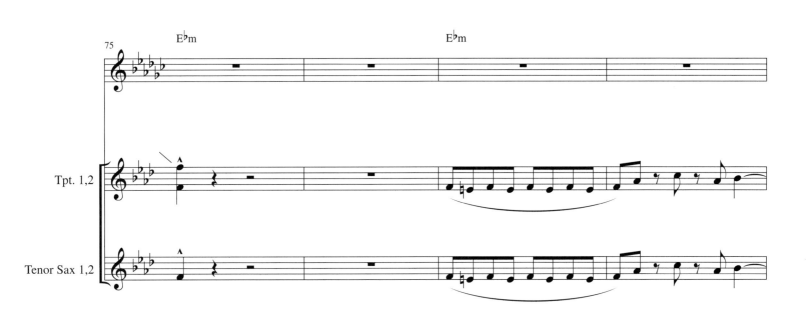

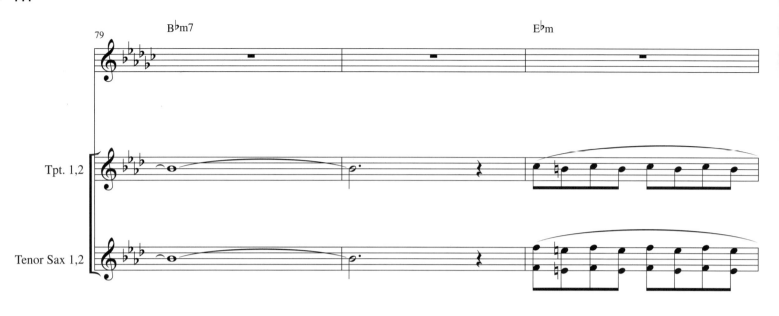

you, got to have you, child. Great God in

heav - en, you know I love you.

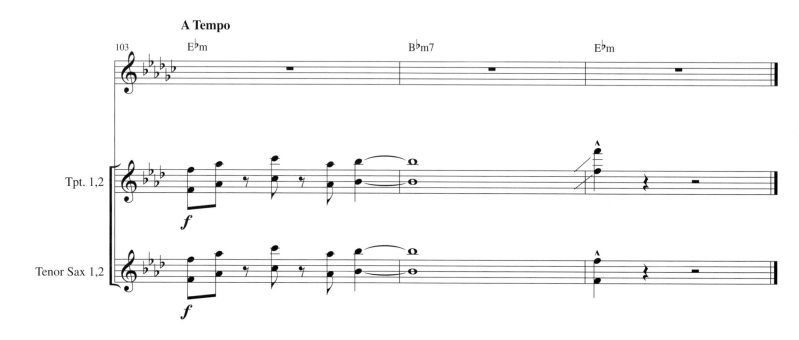

WILL IT GO ROUND IN CIRCLES

Words and Music by BILLY PRESTON
and BRUCE FISHER

Copyright © 1973 ALMO MUSIC CORP. and IRVING MUSIC, INC.
Copyright Renewed
All Rights Reserved   Used by Permission

Additional Lyrics

2. I've got a story, ain't got no moral.
   Let the bad guy win ev'ry once in a while.
   I've got a story, ain't got no moral.
   Let the bad guy win ev'ry once in a while.
   Chorus

3. I've got a story, ain't got no moral.
   Let the bad guy win ev'ry once in a while.
   I've got a story, ain't got no moral.
   Let the bad guy win ev'ry once in a while.
   Chorus

4. *Instrumental*

ZOOT SUIT RIOT

Words and Music by
STEVE PERRY

Copyright © 1998 Sony/ATV Music Publishing LLC and Toilet Brain Music
All Rights Administered by Sony/ATV Music Publishing LLC, 8 Music Square West, Nashville, TN 37203
International Copyright Secured   All Rights Reserved

Who's   that   whis - per - in'
whipped   up,   jit - ter - bug - gin',

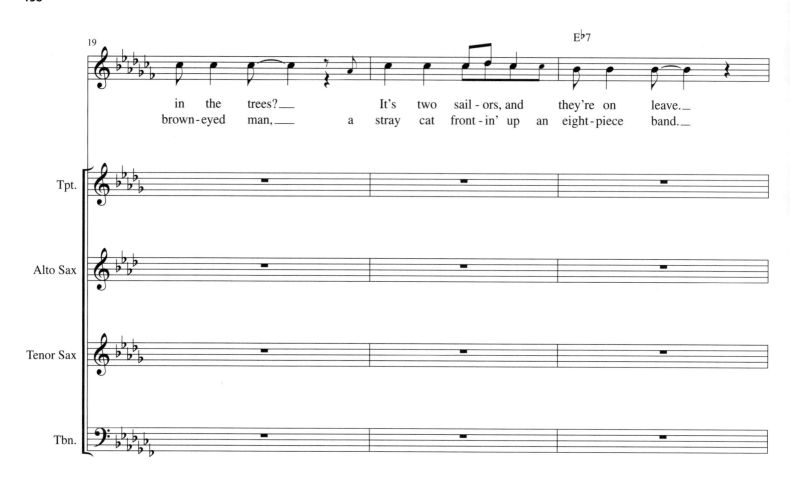

To Coda

when the push - ers come— to shove.———
where your wom - en come— for love.———

Zoot suit ri - ot.   Throw back a bot - tle o' beer.—

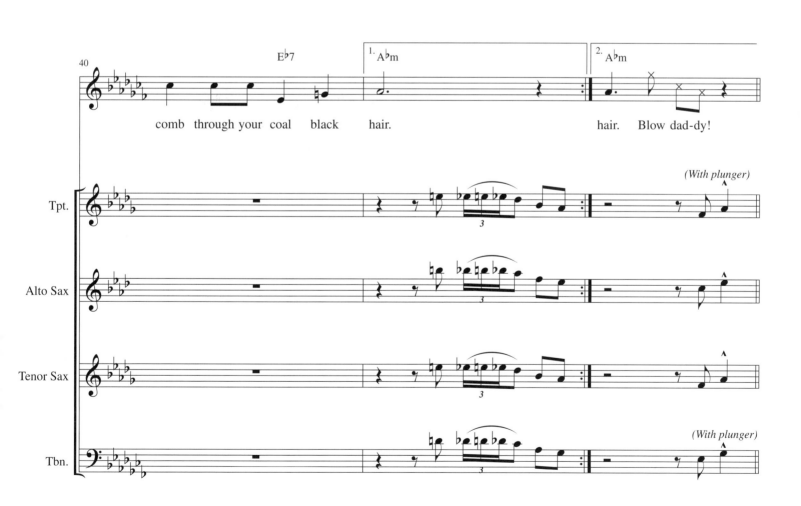

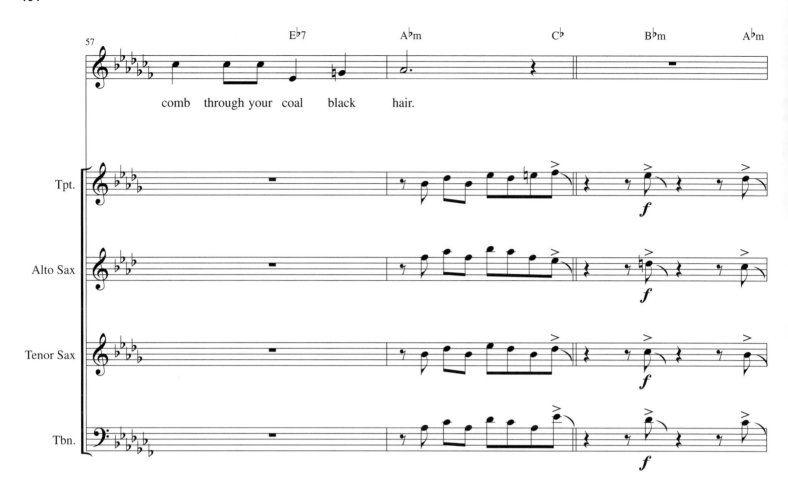

comb through your coal black hair.

You're in a zoot suit ri - ot._____

You're in a zoot suit

ri - ot.

You're in a zoot suit ri - ot._____

A-pull a comb through your coal black hair.

hair.

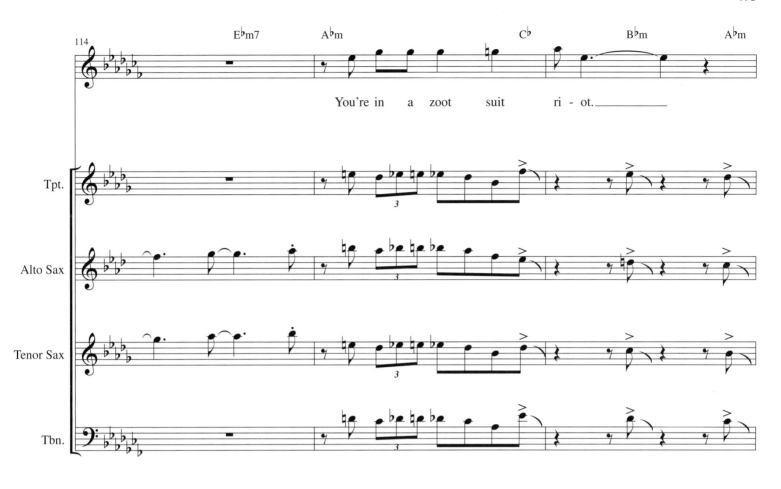

ri - ot._____

You're in a zoot suit ri - ot._____

(Think I'm about ready to sing it...)

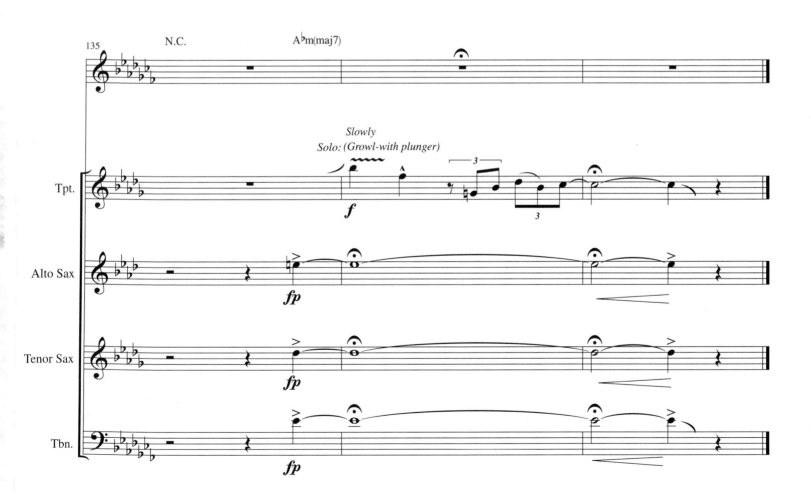

Imagine playing the exact parts of some of the most memorable and consequential songs of our time note-for-note, exactly as the legends played them. This unique new series features transcriptions of all the horn parts included on the original recordings.

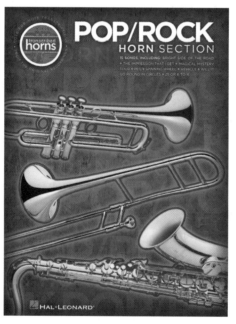

FUNK/DISCO HORN SECTION

15 classics: Brick House • Disco Inferno • Dr. Funkenstein • Fire • Give It to Me Baby • Hold On I'm Comin' • Lucretia Mac Evil • Papa's Got a Brand New Bag • Pick up the Pieces • Serpentine Fire • Superstition • That's the Way (I Like It) • Y.M.C.A. • You Should Be Dancing • What Is Hip.
_____00001148 ....$19.95

POP/ROCK HORN SECTION

15 great hits: Bright Side of the Road • Higher Love • Hot Hot Hot • The Impression That I Get • Jump, Jive An' Wail • Livin' La Vida Loca • Magical Mystery Tour • Peg • Smooth • Spinning Wheel • Sussudio • 25 or 6 to 4 • Vehicle • Will It Go Round in Circles • Zoot Suit Riot.
_____00001149 ....$19.95

R&B HORN SECTION

15 R&B standards: Cut the Cake • Dancing in the Street • Gimme Some Lovin' • Hallelujah I Love Him So • Hard to Handle • I Got You (I Feel Good) • In the Midnight Hour • It's Your Thing • Knock on Wood • Mustang Sally • September • Sir Duke • Soul Finger • Soul Man • You've Made Me So Very Happy.
_____00001147 ....$19.95

FOR MORE INFORMATION, SEE YOUR LOCAL MUSIC DEALER, OR WRITE TO:

HAL•LEONARD®
CORPORATION

7777 W. BLUEMOUND RD. P.O. BOX 13819 MILWAUKEE, WI 53213

www.halleonard.com

Prices, contents and availability subject to change without notice.